Willing and ABLe
Always Be Learning

Ben Sillem

Illustrations by
Ali Imran

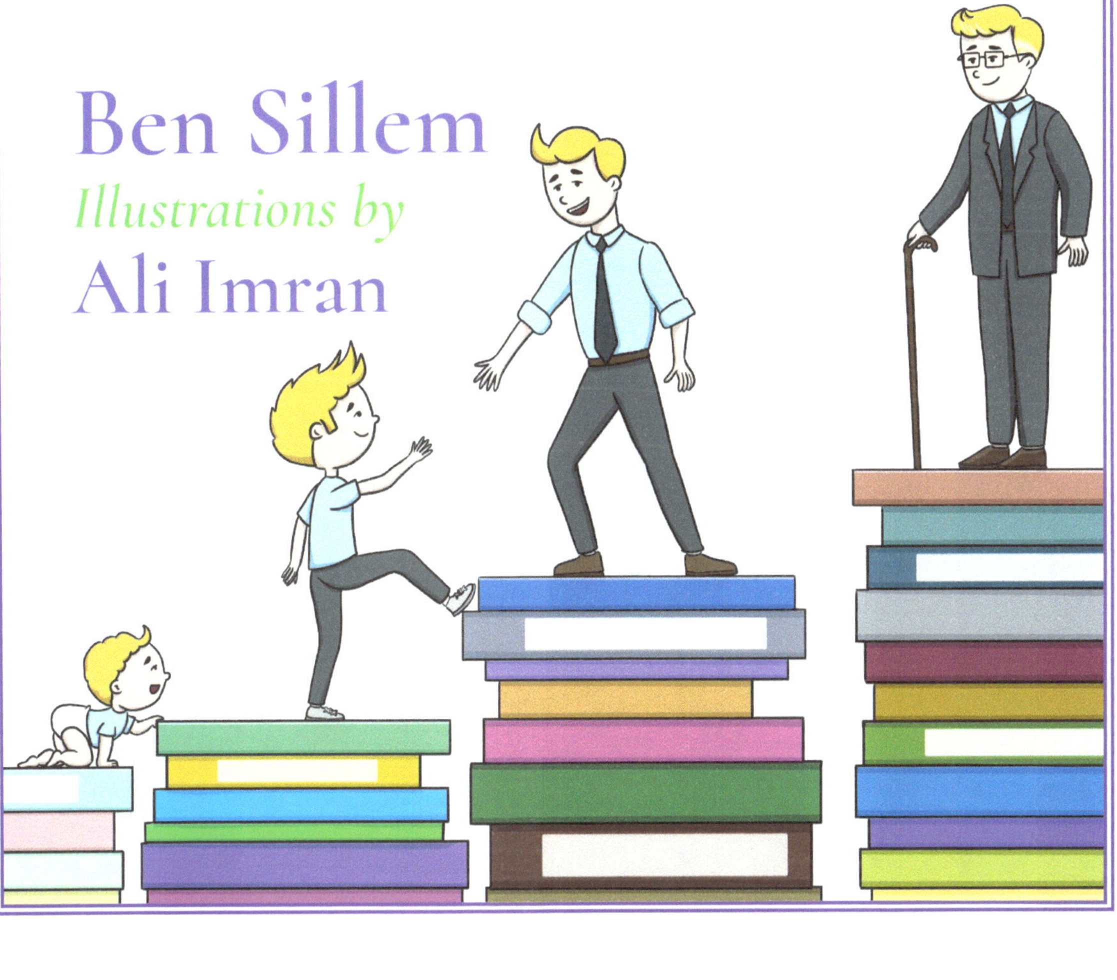

Copyright 2023 © Ben Sillem

All rights reserved. This book or any portion thereof may not be reproduced or used in any manner whatsoever without the express written permission of the publisher except for the use of brief quotations in a book review.

Publisher: Ben Sillem
Contact: bsillem@brokerbuilder.ca

ISBN: 978-1-7782196-3-4 (softcover)
ISBN: 978-1-7782196-4-1 (eBook)

Illustrations by Ali Imran

Cover and page design, layout, and typesetting by
Jan Westendorp/katodesignandphoto.com

First Printing, 2023

This book is dedicated to

Those who understand

Knowledge puts them in demand.

Willing and ABLe

Always Be Learning

Learning, you'll come to see

Is how you become all you can be.

An interest captured does ignite

A desire to learn that does delight.

Reading, writing, and arithmetic

Are all terrific

Let's dot our I's, cross our t's,

And make learning part of our identity.

In Math we practice to calculate

In English we learn to articulate

 These skills we must demonstrate

Before we can graduate.

As you grow

What you know,

Your new strength
you'll be able to show

By how much
further you can go.

When you learn to use your pen as a sword,

Of reading and writing you won't be bored.

Become more proficient with words,

So you'll increase the chance of being heard.

As you pile your knowledge into a mound,

On a subject you'll be able to expound.

Others will listen to your sound

As what you offer is profound.

A great teacher sows the seeds

Encouraging you to
pick up a book and read.

They show the path
for you to lead

How learning is what you need.

Close your mouth, open your ears.

 Your teacher's message
you want to hear.

 Paying attention
helps you see clear.

 Focus, for your learning to steer.

School isn't something to hate.

Learning can be our best mate.

Through its gate

We must pass to matriculate.

Go to school.

 Become a useful tool.

 Avoid spending time with fools.

 Wasting time pretending to be cool.

University, college,
or a trade,

 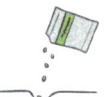

All are places to
make the grade.

Any one of these may be
where your future is made.

So, too, can reading
alone in the shade.

Today, choose to take a look

 At some kind of book.

 If it's interesting,
you'll soon be hooked.

 Eagerly turning pages
nestled in your nook.

There is no magic potion

That helps instill a new notion.

 Ignore the fuss and commotion.

Put your head down
and learn with devotion.

Steer clear of shortcuts.

There's no ifs, ands, or buts.

Forget hocus pocus.

It's not magic. You've got to focus.

Did I forget to mention

That how, what, where, and why
are the start of many a question?

Any of these are great
to act with intention.

Questions guide
your comprehension.

More information seek to imbibe.

The thrill of learning is quite a ride.

A sure-fire strategy
to become a sage

Is to seek a subject
with which to engage.

When you find something
in which to enroll

The pursuit of
knowledge is no toll.

Selecting a subject just for me

Makes learning fun
for its autonomy.

When I pick what I
want to learn and see,

I'm right where I want to be.

Please tell me how
it is up high

That the color blue
comes to be the sky?

Admiring its beauty
makes me smile and sigh.

An answer to this
question could you try?

Sunrise or sunsets,

 Which of nature's wonders
have you not yet met?

 No matter what
it is you study,

 It's more fun doing
it with a buddy.

When you look up at the stars,

Do you dream of learning about Mars?

For some of the world's wonders to unravel,

You'll have to make time to travel.

Learning about the Paleolithic

Can seem pretty darn terrific.

From the fountain of facts drink

To become better at how to think.

 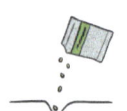   

Will you study
ballistics or statistics?

Do you prefer to learn
the history of mystics?

Paramount, catamount,
or tantamount

Which one of these may
involve something to count?

   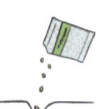 

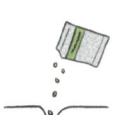

Should you want to extend
your knowledge's reach,

Give thought to whom
else you could teach.

One way to connect
concepts like a suture,

Is to become
someone else's tutor.

Will you write with
a pseudonym?

Homonyms, synonyms,
and antonyms,

Choose one of these to begin

A search for its definition.

The science of neuroplasticity

Confirms the power
of you and me.

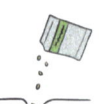

The future of our capability

Is determined by our
willingness to study.

Should you want to
become quite smart,

You've got to be
willing to do your part.

Please take this
message to heart,

And your learning journey
will be off to quite a start.

Daily learning please do diarize.

And take time a formula to memorize.

In due time you'll realize

Even you can start to theorize.

We can never be 100% sure.

Therefore, more
knowledge is the only cure.

Accepting this shows humility

And that's of great utility.

 I hope by now you've come to see

What's true for both you and me

 No matter who we want to be

Learning is what sets us free.

When you make learning fun,

You'll take joy in never being done.

Committing to the long-run

Ensures a King of
knowledge you'll become.

Learning is something
you'd do well to befriend.

It's a skill upon which
you can always depend.

With hard won knowledge
you won't have to pretend.

A brighter future
for you will portend.

To get a good seat at life's table.

You need to be willing and **ABL**e.

Always **B**e **L**earning

And your place you'll be earning.

The End

Where's Joey going next?

Joey learns that saying thanks

Is no prank.

It's alright to be polite.

www.ingramcontent.com/pod-product-compliance
Lightning Source LLC
Chambersburg PA
CBHW050739110526
44590CB00002B/26